- This Arise and Flourish Book Belongs To -

For Layomi, Laolu and Ore

Paperback:	978-1-7399609-0-2
Hardback:	978-1-7399609-1-9
Ebook:	978-1-7399609-2-6

First paperback edition	**August 2021**

Edited by	Dr Tosin Awolalu
Cover art by	INNOENHANCE
Layout by	INNOENHANCE
Illustrations by	INNOENHANCE

Special Credits to **Kemi Tijani**, for sharing her thoughts and ideas on the illustrations during the designing process of her book.

MY FRIENDS ON THE INSIDE

Arise & Flourish

Written By | Kemi Tijani

Illustration by | Innoenhance

Alan is a happy boy. He loves running and playing football. Going to the playground was Alan's favourite thing to do with dad.

One day when Alan finished playing at the playground, he asked, "Dad, what do you think we will be having for dinner"? "I am sure mum will have some lovely yummy food for us," said Dad.

They arrived home and later all sitting at the dinner table; dinner was Pasta and meatballs.
“Mum, why should I eat all this food”? Alan asked, “It has my favourite colour, but it tastes funny. I don't like it 'YUCK.' I like ice cream, cakes and sweets, why can’t I have them instead”?

Alan was upset, and before mum could respond, he got up from the dinner table and went to his room. Dad tried to call him back.

Mum went to Alan's room and explained to him, "you can't have ice cream, sweets and cakes every day; these are just sometimes foods to have as treats"! Alan did not really agree with mum. Alan went to sleep that night without eating his food.

As soon as Alan fell asleep...

He had a dream and found himself in a magical city. All his friends on the inside came alive to help him play, learn and have fun. All his friends, the Heart, Brain, Bone and Muscle, started racing with other friends in the city.

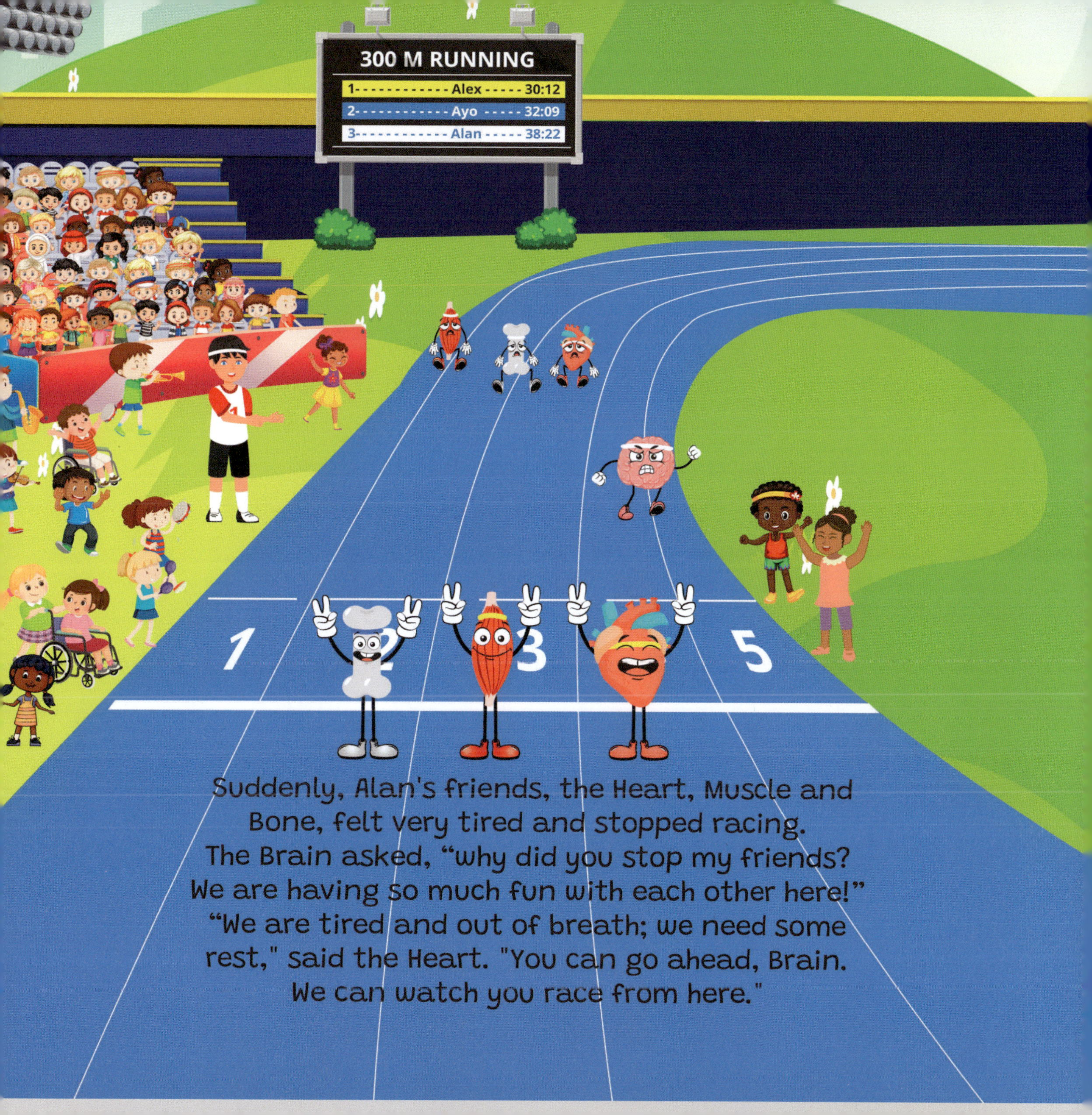

Suddenly, Alan's friends, the Heart, Muscle and Bone, felt very tired and stopped racing. The Brain asked, "why did you stop my friends? We are having so much fun with each other here!" "We are tired and out of breath; we need some rest," said the Heart. "You can go ahead, Brain. We can watch you race from here."

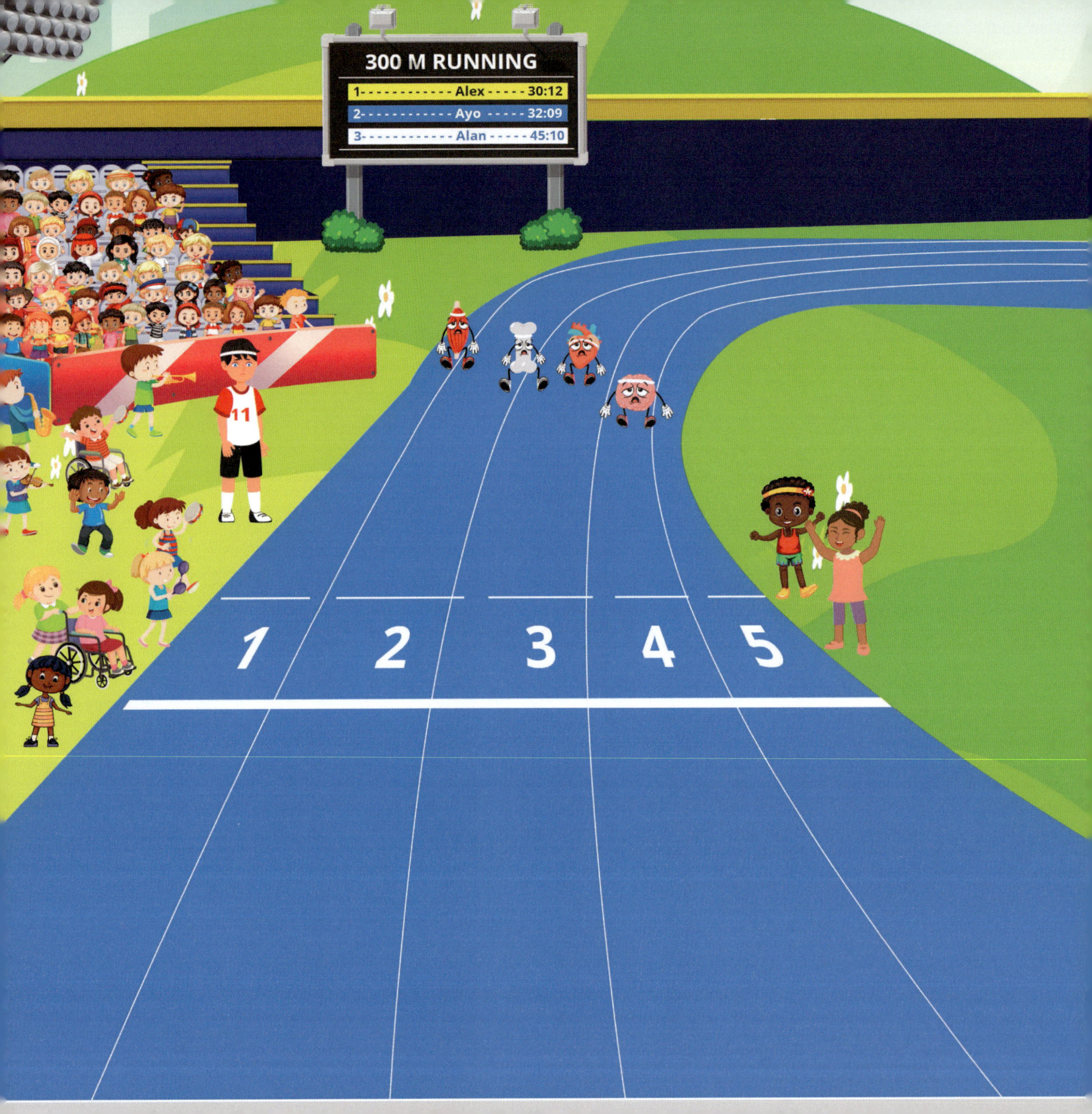
300 M RUNNING
1- - - - - - - - - - - - Alex - - - - - 30:12
2- - - - - - - - - - - - Ayo - - - - - 32:09
3- - - - - - - - - - - - Alan - - - - - 45:10
11
1
2
3
4
5

The Heart breathing heavily, sat
down. Bone and Muscle sat down too.
The Brain answered, “Come on,
friends, I need you all to play; I can't
play without you, my friends, you
know what, I am tired too! We can all
sit down and watch the others," the
Brain said, looking very sad.

"If only Alan would eat less ice cream, cakes, fizzy drinks and sweets, these foods give us energy quickly; it runs out very fast!" said the Brain. "If only he would eat more fruits and vegetables as snacks to nourish us and eat his dinners well in the evening for Mum," said the Heart.

“What can we do?” said the Bone
“Let's talk to Alan,” said the Heart.
“Do you think he will listen?” the Muscle asked.
"We can't sit here and wish we have lots of energy. Let us talk to him." said the Brain. So, all the friends agreed to talk to Alan.

11

The Brain led all the friends to Alan holding hands. The Brain said to Alan, “we are your friends on the inside," all the friends smiled and nodded, “you can't see us, but we are always with you," You can feel us sometimes."

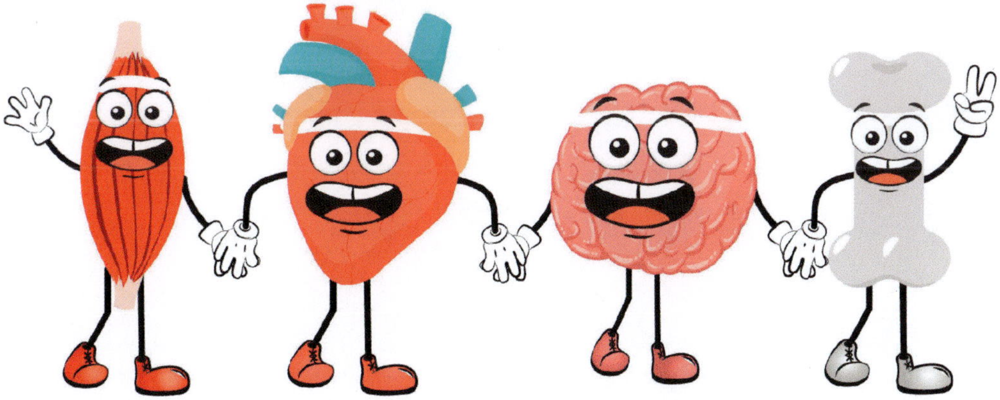

The Heart said, “I help you pump blood and supply oxygen to the other friends; you can feel me when you touch your chest; that is where I live."

The Brain said, “I help you think and talk and guide the other friends too; I live in your head."

The Bone said, "Muscle and I help you to walk, run, jump, dance, ride your bike and kick the ball; you can feel me by touching your hands, legs and fingers."

"We work together to take care of you on the inside. But we need your help on the outside," said the Brain.

'WOW!' said Alan “so nice to meet you, my friends on the inside." "What can I do to help?” asked Alan, very excited to meet his friends.

The Brain said, "we need you to eat your food, including fruits, vegetables, yoghurt and drink lots of water every day to help us work properly. You can have a treat of sweets, biscuits, chocolate sometimes," said the Heart.

"WHY?" Alan asked
"I don't like fruits or
vegetables, and water is
boring," he protested.

"You see, Alan, you may not like fruits and vegetables, but we need it to be strong and healthy. When we are strong and happy, you will be strong and happy too. We can help keep the bad guys away like infections that cause sickness and diseases when your friends the immune system is strong," said the Brain.

“I can help pump blood and oxygen
to all my friends,” said the Heart.

“I can help you run faster and longer when
you are strong," said the Bone and Muscle.

"I can help you think faster and
bring memories," said the Brain.

"We are relying on you to make the right choice of food you send to us; we cannot do it ourselves; we need you, and you need us."

The alarm clock woke Alan before he could answer his friends.

He could smell the scrambled eggs and pancakes being cooked in the kitchen. He got up from his bed, got dressed, brushed his hair and headed out into the kitchen.

"Good morning, mum," said Alan, "from today, I will eat all my fruits and veggies; please remind me when I forget. My friends on the inside need my help to make me a happy, healthy boy." This put a big smile on his mum's face, "who are your friends on the inside?" asked mum, "it's a secret," said Alan smiling back at mum.

Not every day
HIGH IN SUGAR/SALT/FAT
FATS & OILS
Small amounts
2
SERVINGS/DAY
PROTEIN SOURCES
MILK
MILK, YOGHURT & CHEESE
3
SERVINGS/DAY
5-7
SERVINGS/DAY
WHOLEMEAL CEREALS & BREADS
3-5
SERVINGS/DAY
FRUITS AND VEGETABLES

NOW DRAW YOUR FAVOURITE FRUITS AND VEGETABLE

Dear Reader,

Thank you for your purchase, I hope you love reading this book, if you do, please leave a review on Amazon, your reviews will help other families and educators discover “My Friends on the Inside” and I look forward to reading all your reviews. Thank you in advance.

Kemi Tijani

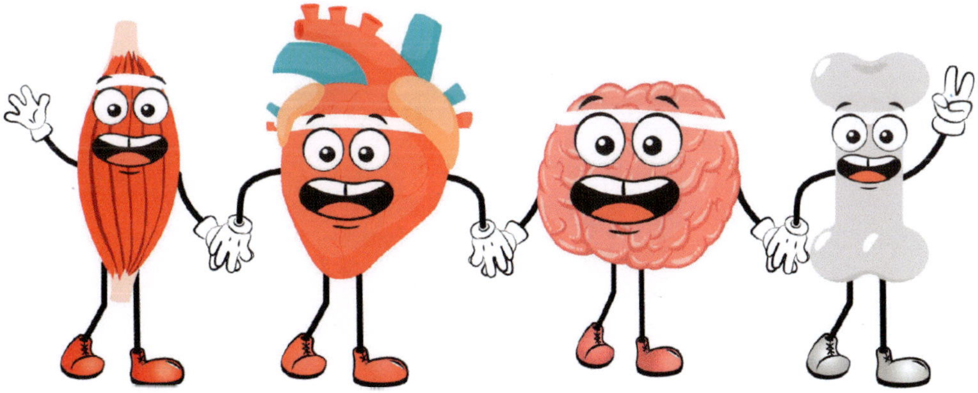

Printed in Great Britain
by Amazon

83967354R00018